Quick Trip

by Jennifer Franklin

illustrated by Erin Eitter Kono

Val and Jeff will go on a
quick trip.

Jeff has a map.
Val and Jeff plan the trip.

Val will fix a snack.
She packs it in a box.

Jeff must pack a bag.
He zips it.

Jeff is packing bags in the van.
They will stop to get gas.

The green van zips past trucks.
Trucks buzz past the van.

Jeff and Val slip in.
Stan and Fran jump and clap!